HOW THE POTATO CHIP WAS INVENTED

DANIEL M. SHAPIRO

sunnyoutside
Buffalo, NY

Acknowledgments

Thanks to the editors of the publications in which these poems, sometimes in different form, have appeared: *Atticus Review; Barge Journal; Camel Saloon; Chiron Review; Convergence; decomP magazinE; The Dead Mule School of Southern Literature; The Entroper; Escape into Life; Forklift, Ohio; Gargoyle; Horse Nihilist; > kill author; Menacing Hedge; Pedestal Magazine; The Prose-Poem Project;* RHINO; *Rufous City Review; Screaming Seahorse; Sentence; Used Furniture Review; Vector;* and *Weave Magazine.*

ISBN: 978-1-934513-40-8
Library of Congress Control Number: 2013957014

sunnyoutside
PO Box 911
Buffalo, NY 14207
USA

www.sunnyoutside.com

KLK

Contents

I

Bob Dylan on the Set of a Victoria's Secret "Angel"
Commercial, Venice, 2004   13

Richard M. Nixon Attends *Star Wars* Premiere,
Brea Mann Theatre, 5/25/77   14

Jackson and Peters   15

First Day of Recording *From Elvis in Memphis*,
1969   16

How the Potato Chip Was Invented   17

Thomas Edison's Favorite Invention   19

Music for the Rapture, 5/21/11   21

How to Write a Score for *The Adventures of Robin
Hood* without Korngold's Help   22

Glynis Johns: The Authorized Biography   24

Re-recording Fleetwood Mac's *Rumours* on its 10th
Anniversary, Hollywood, 1987   26

Characters   27

Independent Film   28

Archibald Discovers Air   29

Archibald Determines the Solution: Rosanna
Arquette   31

II

Gene Rayburn, Host	35
Language Acquisition	36
Bobby Van, Upper Left	37
Match Game '73	38
Brett Somers, Upper Middle	40
Match Game '74	41
Charles Nelson Reilly, Upper Right	42
Match Game '75	43
Elaine Joyce, Lower Left	44
Match Game '76	45
Richard Dawson, Lower Middle	46
Match Game '77	47
Fannie Flagg, Lower Right	48
Match Game '78	49
From the Cards of the Big Three	50
Match Game '79	52

III

Metallica Records Its Debut Album in Rochester,
NY, May 1983   55

Directions   57

Incarnations of the Lynette "Squeaky" Fromme
Action Play Set   58

The Silent Circle   60

Police Reopen Natalie Wood Case, 11/17/11   61

"New Photos of the Fab Four Surface," MSNBC
Video, 7/10/11   63

Julia Roberts and Tom Hanks in *Murder-Suicide*   64

Edouard Manet's "Portrait of Stéphane Mallarmé"
(1876)   65

Chuck Mangione, PIT-ROC, Thanksgiving 1988   67

Fred Astaire Joins The Black Eyed Peas for an
Encore, Staples Center, Los Angeles, 10/11/09   68

Soundtrack of a Strike, 8/3/81   69

Had the Roles Been Reversed, Washington, DC,
12/21/70   70

Bain & Company's Willard Mitt Romney at Studio
54 on Its Second Day, New York, 4/27/77   71

Beowulf, Texas   73

On the Morning Shift at Graceland, 8/16/77   74

Max von Sydow Goes Shopping at IKEA,
    Stockholm, 1994   75

Thomas Kinkade Drops by Andy Warhol's Grave,
    Bethel Park, Pa., 2/22/07   76

Dave Grusin Invents the Quintessential 1980s Film
    Soundtrack   77

Dress Rehearsal for James Brown's Memorial
    Service, Augusta, Ga., 2006   78

Don Knotts Returns to His Hometown of
    Morgantown, W.Va., 1982   79

Klaus Kinski and Werner Herzog Play Yahtzee,
    Machu Picchu, 1972   80

Meeting Poets (Unreleased Brian DePalma Thriller,
    ca. 1977)   81

Squatch Door   82

Brian Wilson Begins to Compose "Good Vibrations"
    outside Dripping Cave, Calif., 1966   83

John Carpenter Splices Two of His Recent Films,
    Los Angeles, 1979   85

David Gregory Fills in for Matt Lauer on *Today*,
    5/11/07   86

The Andrew Lloyd Webber Lecture, Colorado
    Springs Fine Arts Center, 4/1/89   88

Reading Comprehension Segment from Verbal SAT,
    1984   89

1

People who need people are the
luckiest people in the world.

—Bob Merrill

People who need people are
the stupidest of people.

—John Lydon

Bob Dylan on the Set of a Victoria's Secret "Angel" Commercial, Venice, 2004

I see a lady in wings in the wings. Women like her, like that girl over there in the robin's egg blue underwear, they used to move my Blind Willie McTell records from bed to floor, slither in beside. I could outrhyme undreamt-of rappers. Nowadays, Walt Whitman himself would struggle to get in a girl's pants, if girls were ever his thing. The press was half right: These underwear folk give me not only money—they give me another murky dot for the cordoned biography. Though I won't mind leaving this town. Even you must know that line about water, water everywhere. Coleridge and the albatross. I bet you didn't know Coleridge wanted to start a utopian society along the Susquehanna River. I would've written a song about that, but by the time I read it, the counterculture had already discovered the 401(k). Damn. Sorry. The director is telling me to keep my mouth shut. I need to get ready to hear the word *action*.

Richard M. Nixon Attends Star Wars Premiere, Brea Mann Theatre, 5/25/77

Hell-bent on seeing the latest space movie, he insists on standing in a line infested with kids. Pat and he are the last to be let in before a velvet rope separates theatre from tears. Nixon rekindles his love affair with the dark, which stalls in the headlock of John Williams's brash score. He watches backstory scroll across the screen. *Words*, he grumbles. *No one reads more than I.* Scenes ahead, he cringes: *Christ. I finally make it to the movies, and some girl in a sheet is making tapes. Goddamn tapes on a robot.* Deeming Skywalker a long-haired sissy, he waits for a positive, taking in exotic characters that remind him of trips overseas. Finally, he beams as Vader tenses up his fist to cut off a minor character's breath. He mumbles to Pat: *Now that's something that could've come in handy.* Seconds later, Vader releases his grip as an afterthought, a defiant wave.

JACKSON AND PETERS

Most of us focus on only one: the King of Pop, first jittery in bed, clad in a cheap T-shirt with piano keys. Later he'll own the streets in red jacket with sleeves pushed up, silver studs, a zipper for every dance move. He pleads Sharks and Jets to trade switchblades for pliés. The second Michael—all macho in dark sunglasses, red-lined white leather with dragon appliqué—struts with his head tilted back. We never see his eyes. This Michael taught the other one all the steps, went on to craft the shuffles of zombies, to train blind ballerinas to hit their marks. Both Michaels are dead now, the more prominent still mourned through tributes, collector's editions, licensed memorabilia approved by the estate, while the influence of his choreographer speaks through headset microphones as the singers of today pinpoint in tandem, each movement a stone left on his grave.

FIRST DAY OF RECORDING FROM ELVIS IN MEMPHIS, 1969

On film, his pretty-boy water-skier resonated more than the boxer who stood up to gangsters. He whiled away his army time, chronically queasy, karate and amphetamines the sole remnants of basic training. But now he's really done it, having the omnipresent entourage ejected from the studio. *Let him fall on his ass,* The Colonel advises over the phone in impressionist drawl. Sidemen would later reflect on Elvis's drive, the consummate work ethic, how he had relished the stripped-down arrangements, demanded only the finest songs. Artifice would have to wait crestfallen in twenty-three rooms a short limo ride away.

How the Potato Chip Was Invented

The true story sprang from the relationship be-
tween Commodore Cornelius Vanderbilt and cook
George Crum in Saratoga Springs, N.Y. Vander-
bilt, no more a real commodore than Lionel Rich-
ie, was the great-something-or-other of Anderson
Cooper, who tells true stories on CNN. Crum,
who was a Native American, fried some potatoes
for the commodore, who—unlike Sunday morn-
ing—became uneasy when he found the taters too
thick and subsequently sent them back. Like those
irate cooks you see on reality TV shows, Crum
must've muttered something under his breath;
keep in mind this was the mid-1800s and in a
town that would become known for giving birth
to Don McLean's "American Pie," so the cook
likely said, *Who the fuck does this guy think he is?*
Unfortunately, the answer to his question was, *a
fucking Vanderbilt, fuckface, so watch your ass.* Crum
(a name marginally better for a cook than Johnny
Rat-Infested) nonetheless demonstrated his mas-
tery of Caucasian culture by engaging in passive-
aggressive behavior: He cut the commodore's po-
tatoes wafer thin (or as thin as Anderson Cooper's
sexuality-privacy veil, if you are offended by the

religious connotations of the word "wafer"), threw them in the fryer (more likely dropped them gently in the fryer, because throwing things into hot oil is about as brilliant as the lyrics to "Say You, Say Me"), and delivered them to the commodore, who loved them so much he gave Crum his own line of designer jeans and helped to invent that pillar of American society, obesity. This defining moment would become known as "the day the music died."

Thomas Edison's Favorite Invention

There is always a precedent. Our wizard translated Mozart's *Eine kleine Nachtmusik*, stole its proto-macho allegro. Edison told Mary Stilwell, *I can bring you the sun at night.* He said, *I made something that lets us look under our skin. I'll keep working on it until we can see each other's souls.* She married him at sixteen, died of unknown causes before she could turn thirty.

A year later, Edison invited Mina Miller to his place to make what he called "motion pictures." She refused. He said, *No, really. All you have to do is walk toward me; I'll show you what I mean about your walk.* She refused again. *OK,* he said. *At least come to the bar. You've got to see this thing at the bar.* Relenting, she accompanied him to the place, which she found gauche, the place named for a famous singer. She felt the crunch of peanut shells under her embroidered boots, recognized the twang that accompanies a High Victorian dance. *Watch this,* Edison said as he pressed a button that stirred a mechanical bull into motion. He pressed the button again to stop the bull, said *Get on,* pressed it again. Mina would become Wife No. 2.

In 1906, Edison bought his birthplace home in Milan, Ohio, which, unfortunately, is not Cleveland Heights, birthplace of Debra Winger. The last time Edison visited the home, he found it was still lit by gas and candles, as the male ends of wires fumbled through walls.

Music for the Rapture, 5/21/11

Blondie somehow succumbs to Anita Baker in a comic-book caption of almond-scented light. The sky turns a purple shade of Muzak, like a dying tulip's interior. Finally, the one they had all been waiting for arrives: Mavis Staples, in a Vera Wang dress made for the occasion. *She will take us there*, the masses cry, as she rekindles the famous song recorded in Alabama, part of which sits in rubble weeks after tornadoes killed scores. *Grab hammers and nails*, Staples demands in gospel cadence. *We're not finished yet.*

How to Write a Score for The Adventures of Robin Hood without Korngold's Help

Hear the cries of chromatics bouncing off the high ceilings of a castle, freewheeling runs of woodwinds, first slinking over halls, then flitting down staircases without rails. Next, purchase a broadsword perfectly straight as the neck of a quarter note. Tweak it with the nail of an index finger. Listen to the ring, piccolo slice of lethal tuning fork. Shop around for a well-worn bow. Its arrows must be much younger, mimicking the chiseled visage of Flynn in his twenties. Shoot your entire arsenal through body armor and balsa wood. Transcribe the whir and thwack to drum rolls on a gilded timpani. Pay particular attention to the fashions—Norman and Saxon in early Technicolor. A clarinet dabs green on Sir Robin's hat, finishing a passage with feather to brim. Silver fabric glistens against Marian's neck, caressing the fantasy skin of de Havilland, legato lines blown gently through a glass flute. Now comes the unpleasant part, the gloating villainy—cacophonous trios among trombone, trumpet, and oboe standing in for Prince John, Sir Guy, and the sheriff. When the dark whines and bellicose bleats assume the huddled poses of guillotines, you'll know it is time, time to introduce the righteous violins, the violas longing to grow portly, ready to gorge on mutton overdue. Return briefly to the broadsword. Raise the blade to fight nemesis cadenza, the stinging voice of Sir Guy sideswiping Robin's ribs, tingling. Thrust major key into clamor, spry green of a solo trumpet singing joyously, leaving its darker foil wheezing through a crimson mute. Blend victorious horn into brass-section unison, and you'll yield to emotion: leaping fanfares, lilting ballads, fare suitable for peasants granted freedom, hero and heroine standing at the altar side by side in parallel lines, lines that mark the sheet music's end.

GLYNIS JOHNS: THE AUTHORIZED BIOGRAPHY

Googling will get you to the first round of the Most Beautiful Actress Netbrawl, where Glynis Johns was brutally skewered by hyena-faced Miriam Hopkins. (Pity poor Lee Meriwether, who had to contend with the pesky man-to-man defense of Grace Kelly.)

I have watched *Mary Poppins* 37 times. The last 36 times, I have fast-forwarded through most of it, pausing and slo-moing only to gaze into Glynis Johns's bare mole that smolders on her left temple, a mole usually covered by makeup artists during those prudish Golden Times. Meanwhile, all eyes were on Julie Andrews, bringer of evil.

What about the 1956 Pulitzer Prize for Photography, indeed, won by the *New York Daily News* after a punk with a camera strolled outside his office and took a picture of a plane crash. Yet "Glynis Johns, with Her 1956 Thunderbird" went largely unnoticed. In it, she stands behind the intimidating driver's-side door, her left arm bent sharply to apply pressure, to avoid getting trapped in the jaws. (O, to be those jaws.) Her hair is of course windswept.

When *Mary Poppins* got its ass handed to it by *My Fair Lady* at the Oscars (save for best actress winner Andrews, bringer of evil), some Russian-born French actress with a summer home in Canada won for best supporting actress. She had co-starred in *Zorba the Greek*, an admirable lust-for-life lesson woefully devoid of moles.

On the short-lived TV show *Glynis*, our raison d'etre played a mystery writer who, along with her lawyer husband, solves crimes. Together, they go after all the people who have wronged her or may wrong her someday: Julie Andrews, bringer of evil; the *New York Daily News*; that "Zorba" lady; Genghis Khan; Donny and/or Marie; and Maurice Sendak. The show was to be called *Miriam* before Miriam Effing Hopkins backed out at the last minute.

RE-RECORDING FLEETWOOD MAC'S RUMOURS ON ITS 10TH ANNIVERSARY, HOLLYWOOD, 1987

Ike Turner showed up, as did Sonny and Cher, but Tina never returned the calls. An exec had invited them to redo the classic, replete with new set of broken-up couples. Phil Spector would offer up Wall of Sound splendor the original had lacked. At first, the session crept. Following "creative differences" accompanied by brandished weapon, the studio became sad cavern for only Sonny, Cher, and Phil. Dozens of top-notch vets and The Van Nuys Community Orchestra had to be brought in to offset the lost charisma of Ike. The mood allegedly improved after the producer found a perfectly tuned triangle. *This will be my best ever*, thought Spector, as backup singers in red leather skirts rehearsed "The Chain."

CHARACTERS

British actors form a line inconspicuous as the Great Wall. They chitchat politely as they wait to be turned into Chinese terrorists. Accents occasionally drift from understated native to exaggerated Asian. Makeup artists greet them one by one, thanking them in advance for their patience, knowing they'll be sitting still while the artists apply putty under brow ridges to transform eyelids. Yellow will be blended into faces, but not too much, just enough to make the skin seem more exotic than London winters allow. Hours later, half the group, which had looked alike pre-makeup, will look a different sort of alike. In one scene, two rows of actors will stand parallel to each other, while a third row marches perpendicular to them. The formation will resemble a character in Mandarin that has several meanings, including *group* and *offend*.

INDEPENDENT FILM

Ethan Hawke will star as me. Hawke will sit by himself as a lone guitar leaks out a soundtrack. *I remember when the moon still wore velvet curtains,* Hawke will say. During the next three minutes, Hawke will make himself a Manhattan. He will look directly into the camera as he details the drink's various histories, one of which involves Winston Churchill's mother. Knowing no one cares, Hawke will continue. *That was before I hop-scotched across the rising crystal beams,* Hawke will say. Finally, Hawke will look at himself in the bathroom mirror, will survey the creases in his skin, will see the real me as if I were hiding in the medicine cabinet. Backed by one final jagged chord, Hawke will pour a few swallows of Manhattan down the drain in slow motion, the horror blood cherry a sign of things to come.

ARCHIBALD DISCOVERS AIR

The first thing Archibald will tell you when he meets you is The John Wayne Story: Archibald drives his niece to a birthday party—John Wayne's granddaughter's birthday party—but at first, Archibald does not know who this girl's grandpa is. He wants to do a quick drop-off so he can go shopping. And he does. But when he arrives to pick up his niece, The Duke is there blowing up balloons for kids to take home. Archibald begins to weep or giggle uncontrollably. (This is the only part of the story he varies upon retelling.) Archibald's niece couldn't care less about some old cancerous SOB hacking and puffing and spitting into a party favor. None of the children take a balloon home—but Archie does. He clutches the steering wheel one-handed so he won't have to let go of the balloon. He contemplates showering with the balloon but worries hot water might spoil it. He places it on the kitchen table and eats his fruit salad next to it. One day into this courtship, John Wayne dies. Archibald watches the daylong film tribute, still clutching the balloon. He is now certain he possesses the only remaining breath of John Wayne. He must research how to preserve this breath, this form of life that outlasts life. He also wonders what it would be like to breathe in the breath. Caressing the balloon for the last time, he drives one-handed to Winterset, Iowa—birthplace of John Wayne. Finally, he lets go and watches it climb into the breeze, where it will leak slowly and painlessly in a deep sigh.

ARCHIBALD DETERMINES THE SOLUTION: ROSANNA ARQUETTE

Archibald now found himself with two goals in life: 1) Find a beautiful woman; 2) Write a pop hit. Only one woman could help do both, what with the betterment she provided Gabriel and 1/6 of Toto. I will stand outside her window and blast my muse-less song via boombox, Archibald resolved, expecting Rosanna to add muse and repeat as necessary. So Archibald invented the gizmo to end all gizmos—the Conscience-Free-Stalker-Hit-Songwriting-Gizmo, with Cloak-of-Handsomeness Accessory. Archibald happened to forget the batteries so seemed destined to languish in prison with nary the one-hit wonder. Yet in the scrum associated with Archibald's not-go-quietly, the Cloak-of-Handsomeness Accessory went airborne, striking Ms. Arquette in her gorgeous 51-year-old head, rendering her the clueless Susan susceptible to Archibald's flawed accessories. Until a songwriter who smacks of pop hits emerges to right the lass's wrongheadedness, Archibald shall meet her all the way, if one catches Archibald's drift.

II

*Like a lot of the genteel game shows
of the post–*Twenty-One *era,*
The Match Game *was revived
and crass-ified in the '70s.*

—NOEL MURRAY

GENE RAYBURN, HOST

It didn't start this way. Remember when we first
met, when we played it straight? I told you it was
a game of judgment, made conversation. An inven-
tion buff, I asked for one besides Edison, and you
knew. I kept the empty spaces chaste: KING OF
_____, SIDE _____. When you
started to lose interest, started to turn the dial to-
ward affairs, amnesia, I upped the ante: *Johnny al-
ways put butter on his* _____. Then you asked
how my microphone could be so long. Thank God
the '70s aren't just the '60s with a new number.

LANGUAGE ACQUISITION

I crawled beside the black and white while Mom
watched, snickered at words, at how words can fit
where they don't belong, at how her favorite per-
formers blushed when put on the spot. She propped
me up on her lap to see and hear them say a phrase
at a time, even one word, after which a bell would
ring. Mom had read a book about the bells we as-
sociate with rewards until only a sound is left.

BOBBY VAN, UPPER LEFT

My parents coached me for this moment. They said, *You were born to be on the stage.* They said, *Let them heckle. They're just jealous. Imagine them all with pie on their faces. We all look the same with pie on our faces.* But here, I get no top hat, no cane. I sit on orange carpet on second-story plywood. Marquee lights circle no names. During commercial breaks, Elaine asks me if I'm OK. She knows I'm not OK. I forget so easily, forget about...the smile. I can go off-color, call all the ladies *honey*, beat B-level with the smile. And how they look so fine in the white cream, tongues stuffed with it, choked, laughing, two rocks for every dirt.

Match Game '73

Too racy for the Game Show Network but fair
game for the Internet, the episode asks a question
so simple, the missing word is on the lips of oh so
many silent players: *The police commissioner said, "I
think Batman and Robin are _____."*

Our contestant Sandy tries to disappear inside her
royal-and-mauve tartan blouse. She grabs her brow,
delighting our sponsor Excedrin. Begrudgingly,
she speaks: *Queer.* Then applause, laughter, relief.
Self-deprecation courtesy of Richard Dawson, in
porn 'stache and sideburns. Gene Rayburn passes
the potato to Bobby Van, who gives Sandy a match
with QUEER on his card. Van's wife Elaine Joyce
displays QUEERS. Another green triangle lights
up for Sandy.

Charles Nelson Reilly of all people gets it wrong.
Dawson and Brett Somers pour on the esoteric,
but Nanette Fabray writes FAIRIES, which of
course counts as QUEERS, as URBAN counts
as BLACKS, as 57 CENTS for women counts
as ONE DOLLAR for men. Before Sandy could
take home a few hundred bucks, more blanks

needed to be filled, entendres doubled, cigarettes relit, large-collared guffaws taped in front of a live studio audience. The era preserves itself with a recorder seemingly everywhere, a small portion of tape to be erased due to constraints of time.

BRETT SOMERS, UPPER MIDDLE

You think of me as that gaudy aunt, that friend of your mom's friend who insists on a kiss, who perfumes you with powder, with gin, Virginia Slims. What big eyes I have, oversized glasses. Cover your ears to block the cackle; I am Snow White's witch who falls off the cliff.

Once I tried it, came to the party without my wig, with eyes naked. No one could see a thing. I just stood there, sipping Coke through a straw. (I didn't even make that bubbly sucking sound at the end.) Finally, I took out an index card and marker, wrote NOTHING in left-handed black to leave a clue, went home to be with husband and costume.

MATCH GAME '74

On vacation from a three-day week, Debbie wore
pigtails, a Laurel and Hardy sweater. Enunciating,
her clean British diction tinkled on the colonel's
shoes. She deftly took down Carol by saying the
droopy-drawered Tin Man NAILED ON his
pants. Baum had blamed industry for turning man
to metal.

A fine mess by Dawson led to a goose egg: NAVY
blue. In the end, she got hatcheted, bypassed
WATERMELON for COCONUT to garnish
King Kong's martini. Stunned, she climbed aboard
the Lazy Susan, peered through the pimento-free
hole while her dead countryman in bowler hat
wept, frantically groping for oil to cut rust.

CHARLES NELSON REILLY, UPPER RIGHT

Each young actor entered stage right, went to the same red plastic chair. *You're on the porch. Savannah, Georgia. Summertime*, he kept crowing. *And don't say a word.* Everyone just sat nervously—as if Savannah summers were agents calling with bad news—waiting to be dismissed with a shout of *Next.* Finally, he gave up, slowly entering stage right to slump on that red chair, to sip lemonade from a tall pantomimed glass, to slap an invisible mosquito with a left hand that transformed into sun visor, under which he glared at the kids on his lawn.

Gene Rayburn, white, to Gregory Morris, black:
Wake up, or we're going to put you in the back of the bus.

A year with so many correct responses—Lennon
Sisters: <u>DRUNK</u> off Welk's bubbles. World Trade
Center fire: Out with <u>WATER</u>. John Mitch-
ell: <u>GUILTY</u>. Carlton Fisk: Ball waved <u>FAIR</u>.
Squeaky Fromme, Sara Jane Moore: <u>DOWN</u> like
Joe Frazier.

Morris: *You can't do that because I own the bus now.*

ELAINE JOYCE, LOWER LEFT

You don't know the stories? *West Side Story*? How I'm really four years younger than they say? It's because I never complain. Bobby used to say I had a voice of wind chimes. When a storm swept through, I still sounded beautiful. He preferred the softer music of bedtime.

I once knew a marathon runner, the least patient person. She always botched the paperwork, her mind on improving the pace of Miles 5 through 9. Bobby was sick for a year, a mere sprint. Until the end he could sing, always, while I stayed bedside remembering the stories, with hardly a wind to speak of.

We cannot blame Gary for what he did, bypassing Dawson. At home, he had Lee Meriwether's picture on his wall, the picture that caught her with one hand cupped mid-swivel, the other holding a bejeweled staff. Later she covered them in gloves with cat's claws, played the scientist trying to save men from time. And those eyes: Were they blue or green? How could he forget? *Come on, dummy: She's right over there. Just look at her.*

Mind now gone, he went with LION'S for _____ CAGE, begging the audience to groan. She wrote down <u>BIRD</u>, smart as hell, always smart as hell, and apologized: *Can I take you to lunch someday and dinner and anything after?* Meanwhile, Dawson, the bastard, curled up silently, the gory smirk of <u>LION'S</u> on his card.

Richard Dawson, Lower Middle

I've been under your breath. I've heard you call me
lapsed Limey, *lecherous lout*, all because of 11 years'
worth of Hampshire-mouth kisses. I risked my
life for those kisses, got death threats and worse:
threats from sponsors to pull the plug. At first,
I planted them on the cheeks of black women,
Asians, even a Pacific Islander. The postcard read,
I'll sprinkle some of you in Samoa. So many men lack
the insight to be self-loathing.

I find that fuck-you kisses taste better, so I switched
to lips, smooched the occasional girl, puckered up
for the whole goddamned melting pot. But every
show began with love, the love between man and
survey, love we find when the masses agree with
us. And we closed with love, sign language, a kiss
through the television without a sound.

Craig got screwed, said <u>SCHOOL</u> was where Dumb Dora sends her cultured pearls. Ed and Brett smartly scrawled <u>COLLEGE</u>, while Charles wrote <u>SCUBA DIVING SCHOOL</u>. Three quick happy dings and Craig seemed on his way. But when Debralee and Richard put <u>FINISHING SCHOOL</u>, the judge said no. Patty put <u>NIGHT SCHOOL</u>, and the judge said no. Three raspberries, and the audience warbled a fight song medley.

Long after the round was over, Debralee and Richard still refused to take down the blue cards, keeping them raised like the black-gloved fists of Tommie Smith and John Carlos on the podium. Debralee and Richard chose to champion the equal rights of similar phrases.

It was all over when Cathy got four matches for <u>HOOKER</u>, the easy answer that giggled on the corner, the answer that sent Craig backstage clockwise with not enough cash to foot the bill.

Fannie Flagg, Lower Right

Hiding behind what her peers called BA-ZOOMS
on the blue cards, she stabbed her fears with Red-
stone bayonets, fears of being exposed. The vilest
of cleavages cut words in her head, left her with
only images of those green tomatoes, people with
names she couldn't spell. Never mind sexuality,
on-air jokes about queers, fairies. So few can truly
write, can teach us how to make up. We don't need
anyone to sketch plots; we crave the flesh of char-
acters, the intimate slivers of ourselves we've gone
too long without finding.

MATCH GAME '78

<u>SERIES</u> became the key word, as they all tripped up when the work got harder. The Vampire of Sacramento made his handprints with the victim's blood, while the Deliberate Stranger blew it, skipped a traffic stop. Near year's end, they even got The Clown. Adding the Star Wheel replaced choice with chance, taking it out of the contestants' hands. When the money stopped coming, they went home to watch *Dallas* on Sylvania Supersets, mounted La-Z-Boys while Big Bad Wolves boiled in Kozy Heat fireplaces. Even the neutron bomb got tucked under covers, eyes and teeth removed before the spinning could stop.

FROM THE CARDS OF THE BIG THREE

1. CNR

When I TAKE MY CLOTHES OFF, my BODY
reeks of BIRD DOODIE, of PATIENTS' OR-
GANS. Hey: It's just a figure of speech. We have
no use for BUST(S) or BLOW while we toss each
other like FRISBEES, TWIGGY. My PELVIC
REGION hops from BED TO BED, POT to
PILLOW.

2. BS

Ladies at the SHOE FACTORY break too long.
They spend more time KNITTING than working.
And can you blame them? They even PLUCK their
FRISBEES from thin air, imagining HOWARD
COSELL on the play-by-play. When the boss
comes, they will hit the DEEP FREEZE, bellies
a-slosh like a WATERBEG [sic].

3. RD

I know a HOOKER who, when she's really on a ROLL, COVERS her NOSE with a PIECE OF CHEESE shaped like a RUBBER DUCK. That's just her thing. Afterward, she binds me with my own TIE, reads me the Gideon BIBLE, her NEWSPAPER.

MATCH GAME '79

When Dawson left, he wrote <u>FARE THEE WELL</u> for the fans. CBS canceled the 1970s without warning, ratings obscured by partial meltdown, hostage crisis. The day it stopped, President Carter fought for his life, wielding canoe paddle to ward off swamp rabbit. On another network, the show would be resurrected without years, without markers to signify specifics. Blanks would shift from beginning to middle to end, their fill-ins stuffed into desolate dressing rooms. Toupees, ashtrays, wide lapels, carpet remnants would all be loaded into prop trunks, donated to middle school theater clubs. Students would sneak in risqué couplings under coats. *You can't do anything else once you do game shows,* Reilly would say, hissing outward bound, baring choppers at the powers that be. *You have no career.*

III

*Famous, adj.: Conspicuously
miserable.*

—Ambrose Bierce

METALLICA RECORDS ITS DEBUT ALBUM IN ROCHESTER, NY, MAY 1983

The four horsemen flashed the lights before techs
could adjust the white/black ratio of sky. In this
land of Chuck Mangione, listening would seldom
go easily.

A studio by the name of Music America knelt be-
hind a green sign with white letters: *The City of
Rochester Welcomes You.* Peeling paint nodded its
long-haired nod at the whiplash-quick thrashers
from the West.

Even boogaloos had to stutter-step. cowering in
the cool basement of the 50-years-dead social club.
The drummer insisted his cymbals rotated from
the callused ghosts.

The sweater-vested man enlisted to engineer had
worked the counter at Music Lovers Shoppe, col-
lected sweaty bills for vinyl at retail price. He
would translate the band's seek-and-destroy riffs
into the soundtrack of zits that couldn't be hidden,
zits that shielded braces, speech mid-voice-change,
threadbare denim or faux leather a daily coin flip,

weed-burned fingers contorting into devil horns.
This would be a symphony for the front window,
an opus to unite the lonely at breakneck speed.

Six weeks later, the band would flee for anesthesia,
for all the gloom-free cities. The tightly gripped
hammer would give way to blood, jump in the fire
midsummer to go three times platinum, a discard-
ed mirror of shrugged-shouldered East Avenue
clouds.

DIRECTIONS

I. To The David Bowie Birthplace and Museum, Brixton

Take Dulwich east past poet streets: Chaucer, Spenser, Shakespeare. If you get to Railton Road, the one where they rioted, you've gone too far.

II. To the Bathroom at The David Bowie Birthplace and Museum, Brixton

With eyes peeled, go between the Plain Suits (1962–1968) and the Plain Suits (1999–   ) on the left. You'll pass through an orange curtain, the intimidating mullet. Brush against the curves of the turquoise door with mauve androgyne stick figure. If you get to the talking lion, you've gone too far.

III. To the Stalls in the Bathroom at The David Bowie Birthplace and Museum, Brixton

Follow the path marked REINVENTION in Helvetica Neue 25 Ultra Light. If you find orgied cocaine or truth, you've gone too far.

Incarnations of the Lynette "Squeaky" Fromme Action Play Set

I. 1971-1974

The one with prototype buzz cut,
X carved into forehead. Twist
the peg clockwise to make her
walk progressively more slowly,
a daze of plastic. The eyes rub off.

II. 1975

Pure vibrancy in a red robe.
Environmental brochure
fits in hand; California State
Capitol sold separately.
(Recalled; gun would not fire.)

III. 1976-2009

A track shuttles Lynette
in the pendulum between
prison cell and courtroom.
(1987 cell defective; known
as "jailbreak version"; valuable.)

IV. 2009-present

Hardest of all sets to find.
(Parole officer figure included.)
Comes with suburban duplex,
safety hazard of defiance removed.
String to voice box jams when pulled.

THE SILENT CIRCLE

Financial weakness spread Universal: In the 1920s, the studio laid waste to a ghastly lot of Lon Chaney films because it needed the silver. The thousand faces burned into celluloid flickered a last time in cooler light. Smiths melted the metal amorphous, twisted in a made-up ghoul's grin. Pristine gangsters vanished, along with unnamable monsters distinctly human. Tales of aging moviegoers recall only the flakes of storylines, the glints of imagery.

The silver could be anywhere now, maybe sitting in a permanent dungeon but perhaps in a ring on display at the jewelry store around the corner. The woman who buys it might find herself making an obscure, fluid gesture, a hand movement she can't explain that takes the place of words.

Police Reopen Natalie Wood Case, 11/17/11

At school the day after, they had made the joke:
What kind of wood doesn't float? They must've
known she was my first, the one I'd taken to prom.
(*Prom* always sounds too short—*promenade* supe-
rior—but *promenade* makes me think of the Prom-
enade Deck from *Love Boat*, and I never want to
think about boats or smiles again.)

I wouldn't have asked her to wear what she'd
worn in *Rebel*, but when I picked her up, she had
it all: the orange-red scarf, the green sweater with
sleeves rolled up, hair prepared for 1955, those
brown eyes prepared to blink at the prospect of
a curse. I had pulled open the passenger door for
her. She scoffed at the idea of a seat belt, knowing
the Chevette wasn't cliff-bound, knowing my lips
provided sufficient protection. When we stepped
into the gym, our song came on: *As the music dies
something in your eyes calls to mind a silver screen and
all its sad goodbyes.* The anchor didn't say if she'd
been found with eyes open.

Who knows if we'll ever discover the truth, the
other men she'd kissed on location while crew-

men were striking the set. Even thirty years after I heard the news, I remain a novice. I cringe at others' accounts of experience, accounts whispered in front of lockers. I still look at the scar between my left middle knuckle and finger where I'd punched the keyhole. Even drunk, I could say the neighbor's dog Maria had bitten me there. The only clue: Maria. I had figured no one would ever believe. But now, as police look again, as they peel away the rouge, the rainbow kimono of 1981, we use our skeleton keys, technology. Someday we will all gather at that planetarium on the hill to look up at stars, constellations on a curved ceiling, constellations named for us.

"New Photos of the Fab Four Surface," MSNBC Video, 7/10/11

Another who-cares headline, we figured, introducing images of the overexposed mid head-bob, black and white yellowed by the long-passed excitement of teenage girls. You spotted it first: A stray photo we were sure no one else saw, trapped between the syllables of Lester Holt's banter. It showed John Lennon clad in black jumpsuit and face-mask, holding a shovel over an open grave. Yoko Ono stood at his side, remnants of a slight smile on her lips. Atop the body, Lennon had placed forty pounds of dirt, staff paper, jar of cranberry sauce, left-handed bass. *It might take a while to find another,* Lennon said, *but the real trick will be getting them not to believe.*

JULIA ROBERTS AND TOM HANKS IN MURDER-SUICIDE

The stars call their agents about the new title. They had signed on to make *Amelia Porter*, a main character's name so a surefire hit flick. Saying the change kills the ending, they begin to steam, Hanks irate no one considered *Tony Porter*. Roberts laughs, deems Hanks "Tony Nobody," accuses him of chauvinism. Hanks retorts, If he's a chauvinist, then she's over forty. *Now we're getting somewhere*, the director gushes.

Edouard Manet's "Portrait of Stéphane Mallarmé" (1876)

The poet's mother wouldn't have nagged him about
that lit cigar in bed. She might've asked why he
needed to wear a peacoat indoors, why he had to
be lazy, so *indolent*, as she'd upgrade. What would
irk her was his glassy-eyed anti-gaze past the open
book. *Don't pretend to read. I'll know.*

> The smoke, real as end rhyme, marks the
> place in text, text to be turned to memories
> in ash as the peacoat conjures an infernal
> symbol rendering firewood rended. (When
> you write "mother" in French, the letters
> spell out "mere.")

*What are you now? 34? 35? You're too old to deny
the pinch of ancestry. Call the physical realm a lens.
Just remember who taught you the alchemy that spins
poverty into an open house, generosity that brings over
Yeats and Rilke every Tuesday night. Slump affectedly
with thumb stuck out of pocket, but you know it's true.*

> I was 34 then, ill at ease to speak literally.
> You were perfect, sedate in the shape of skin.

65

I ran my lines diagonally, spaced my words. You gifted me with rulers, horizontal repair. I ended my epic with letters enlarged, a shout. You never believed it wasn't just a picture.

Chuck Mangione, Pit-Roc,
Thanksgiving 1988

We wouldn't have missed him even more than ten
years after The Blockbuster. Panama hat-assisted,
he must have stood no more than 5½ feet tall. He
had been trying to board, struggling to control the
case that housed the famous horn he embraced
like a newborn on the cover we used to pretend to
mock. In private, we, too, closed our eyes.

Security would flag him down, suspicious of
his fumbling. Frantically he would tell them
not to open the case, which had started to
rise to the ceiling when they snatched it away.
Bracing it, flipping up the clips, they discovered
the secret when a tiny cloud emerged, the well-
kept lure of airplay. He had wanted only to bring
it back home.

FRED ASTAIRE JOINS THE BLACK EYED PEAS FOR AN ENCORE, STAPLES CENTER, LOS ANGELES, 10/11/09

The sampled beats of "The Funky Drummer" explode, grafted onto Irving Berlin's "Change Partners." Taboo and apl.de.ap exit stage right, high-fiving Astaire, who awaits his turn to sing. Auto-Tuned, he woefully serenades Fergie and will.i.am, who portray lovers we hate in a jerky lowbrow grind. Astaire, clad in a wetsuit with track lights, enters on *Ask him to sit this one out*, taps will.i.am on the shoulder, cuts in. The music stops violently. Astaire tears off Fergie's wetsuit with track lights as lasers reveal a lavender evening dress. She returns the strip; Astaire now wears a tuxedo with lavender tie. Music begins again, Auto-Tune removed, string orchestra added. Pink neon flashes an Art Deco number: 1938. Managing to match Astaire, Fergie becomes a backward, high-heeled legend.

SOUNDTRACK OF A STRIKE, 8/3/81

In '64, he flaunted his acting chops. slapping Angie
Dickinson with a non-dominant right. She didn't
want to go, but he tightened those eyelids, said: *You
get back to the hotel and stay there.* Now four months
removed from a bullet near the heart, he juts out
that mad left hand, tells them, *Get back to work or
you're fired.* He'd turned on the radio hours before
the short march of union began. He'd been moved
by a two-day-old tune, a simple sentiment: *Forever,
I'll hold you close in my arms; I can't resist your charm.*
He'd been moved not because of his feelings for
Nancy, not because of Lionel's feelings for Diana,
but by the feelings of those people, those people
drawn to the aw-shucks grandpa. He could say *I
just murdered your mommy, little gal* in that cadence,
and it would still be there, still working. Twelve
years later, some of the ones he'd let go would get
their jobs back, but he would still be winning, still
mumbling about a love that's endless.

HAD THE ROLES BEEN REVERSED,
WASHINGTON, DC, 12/21/70

Both men would've been in suits and ties, with
Elvis smiling awkwardly, reluctant to give Nix-
on a Bureau of Illegal Surveillance Monitoring
badge. The Colonel, that proto-Cheney svengali,
was absent, handling the business in Cuba and
Chile, but this time, the King had the Red But-
ton at the ready, largest rhinestone on the big belt
buckle. After the photo op, Nixon would return
to Yorba Linda, extend a reel-to-reel tape across
the entrance of a school for a ribbon-cutting cer-
emony, warn children about the dangers of tat-
tling. Back at the White House, two-year-old
Lisa Marie would beam in front of the Christmas
tree, under which first lady Priscilla had placed an
oversized dollhouse, replica of a Memphis home
the girl would never know.

Bain & Company's Willard Mitt Romney at Studio 54 on Its Second Day, New York, 4/27/77

Day One wouldn't have worked, what with booze for sale sans license, but today was fair game. *Cranberry juice, please*, he shouts over disco beats and string arrangements, reaching into the right pocket of his Brooks Brothers vest, peeling out a ten-spot. *Keep the change.* Looking up at the ceiling, he is unable to determine what use the Man in the Moon would have for a tiny spoon. When he reaches the room encased in rubber, he removes a Waterman pen and tiny notepad from the left vest pocket, jots down: *Brilliant concept. That would keep our boardroom clean once and for all.* Weaving through colors, he catches his breath before a bearded, shrouded man with a parabola of light emanating from long hair, purple shadow smeared on eyelids. *Don't worry*, the man says. *I'm not who you think I am. Steve is in there.* Pointing a bony finger toward a green door, the man directs thirty-year-old Mitt toward the meeting, where he hopes to consult, to lay the groundwork for financial solvency, to advise how to make the scene without losing your shirt. The room behind the green door appears

tiny but stretches past R-rated, so our man swiftly
exits, wipes four inches of glitter off his Florsheims
before re-entering the Cadillac back to LaGuardia,
while the notebook burns a hole in his pocket.

BEOWULF, TEXAS

In the unreleased film version, Jimmy Stewart scowls directly into the camera as he sums up the mother. *Your son looked nothing LIKE you*, he spits, doing his best to hide the Indiana, Pa., cadence. *He was a little bit... HANDsome. Open casket, for sure.* Reverse shot: Mom reaches under her housedress, grabs the Smith & Wesson, fires a quick one that dents the tin star. (Director Anthony Mann would later call the film *a perfect sequence of a bullet ricocheting off a sheriff's badge, plus whatever the hell James Stewart felt like doing*.) We think we hear only that shot, but Mom falls like a bag of feed. The dust cloud briefly makes the body disappear. Her blood spills Herschell Gordon Lewis heavily, so heavily it would demand reshoots the budget couldn't take, heavily enough to leave a round, cayenne-hued stain on the map.

On the Morning Shift at Graceland, 8/16/77

All he wanted was a glass of water, no food. I gave it to him and he just gulped it down. Usually he would take his time, with a tiny cup. He went upstairs and I got back to cleaning. When I heard that noise, I wasn't scared. He used to break glass a lot back then. Later, when I knew something wasn't right, I sent one of the boys up. I didn't want to go through those black doors.

I remember my first day, when the employment agency told me to drive out to the big house with the musical note. I parked next to the note, went inside, and had the table set before I had even met him. I didn't think I knew who he was then, but I remembered further back to a barefoot boy in overalls playing sloppy guitar, sweet guitar. The streets were blocked off.

MAX VON SYDOW GOES SHOPPING AT IKEA, STOCKHOLM, 1994

Cashing in on the perks of an advertising gig, he imagines what $5,000 worth of furniture would look like in Granddaughter's home. The gent who played chess with Death now faces a difficult decision: Poäng vs. Pello. He remembers assembling the chairs, elapsed-time video compiled to show that it was so simple even the brooding foil of Bergman could build it. He knows what Lafite Rothschild can do to their birch veneers, what lost cabernet can do to man's lifespan. *Ah, piss,* he figures. *She'll take six Extorp Jennylunds in Brunflo red, their removable, machine-washable covers a must-have for Swedish mommies always on the go.* Gently lowering his lanky, 65-year-old frame into an Isunda-gray Karlstad, he recalls the closure of *The Virgin Spring*'s Töre, who blindsided his daughter's murderers in an easy-clean release.

THOMAS KINKADE DROPS BY ANDY WARHOL'S GRAVE, BETHEL PARK, PA., 2/22/07

Keep the car running, Kinkade tells his driver. He climbs the hill, reaches the marker, gropes for the soup can and paperweight in the TK-monogrammed satchel. *Chicken & Stars?* he hisses. *That asshole was supposed to get Tomato. No respect.* With meticulously gloved hands, he places can and weight—radiating with the Thomas Kinkade™ Painter of Light™ logo—atop the stone. *You taught me about objects,* he tells frozen ground before snapping a Polaroid, walking back down the hill. Soon he will return to the studio, clip the photo to canvas, make improvements, eager to excise aboveground pool from background. Referring to Revelation 6:8, he will add the pale horse ridden by Death, rein in the beast thanks to ferocious pastel illumination. *God has instructed me how to make fifteen minutes eternal,* he will muse while dabbing on the final trademark.

DAVE GRUSIN INVENTS THE QUINTESSENTIAL 1980S FILM SOUNDTRACK

The composer crafts his distinctive template, a slick mix of syncopated jazz piano and flawless drumming, freeze-dried gloss to keep Reagan's hair in place. It would synchronize perfectly with Dustin Hoffman's uptight *Tootsie* walk, convince us an unquestionable man could dress up women's lib. It would whittle Henry Fonda's monster dad down to darling old poop, toe-tappingly strip lasting impressions from De Niro and Streep.

As Iran-Contra hearings spew from his TV, Grusin begins to envision the score for *A Dry White Season*, the anti-apartheid coda, black justice defined by white courage. Turning down the sound, he extracts glorious chords from the keyboard, making Oliver North a patriot.

DRESS REHEARSAL FOR JAMES BROWN'S MEMORIAL SERVICE, AUGUSTA, GA., 2006

Bootsy Collins arrives late and has to pay a $100
fine. On stage at the eponymous arena, our star
and his backing band, The Soul Generals, crouch
in a circle to go over choreography and entrances,
the costume changes. An X in black electrical tape
will be placed nearby to show the college president
where to stand for the posthumous doctorate pre-
sentation. Paths will have to be kept clear so na-
chos and pretzels can make their way to mourners.
Well, he thinks, at least the video montage is ready.
I won't be here, Brown barks for the fifth time. *Don't
fuck this up.* He begins to rush everyone as his en-
ergy shifts to New York City, to the other dress
rehearsal. He imagines his body encased in gold,
atop a horse-drawn carriage, en route to the Apol-
lo Theater, where longtime MC Danny Ray will
drape him in a sequined, boy-who-cried-wolf cape.

DON KNOTTS RETURNS TO HIS HOMETOWN OF MORGANTOWN, W.VA., 1982

He left to become the voice and straight man for Danny "Hooch" Matador, to whom he applied Murphy's Oil Soap nightly. A top casting agent would tap him to make Andy Griffith better looking, less awkward. All the while he meticulously adhered to the discipline passed on from his mother, who ran a boarding house. On 1980s TV, he began to permit himself to stretch, to portray a gaudily clad lecher slinging double entendres like hot coals. Today he will receive the key to the city, grand-marshal a parade through his old neighborhood, and visit his father's grave, where alcoholism and schizophrenia labor to decay. Known for bug-eyed double-takes, he is genuinely taken aback when introduced to his alma mater's latest convenience: a personal rail system, which, nondescript in tan windbreaker and tweed cap, he will ride alone until dawn.

KLAUS KINSKI AND WERNER HERZOG PLAY YAHTZEE, MACHU PICCHU, 1972

Petulant cries of native birds slip beside the crunch of dice in a shaker. With two turns left, Kinski appears landslide bound, taunting Herzog, who's nearly 8,000 feet from an upper-level bonus. *These dice—so perfect, so milky white—the inside of a young girl's thigh—*, Kinski purrs as he completes a small straight. Herzog copes by counting fibers of syrupy clouds. He settles for the lowest possible four-of-a-kind score. *Six*, Kinski mutters. *What a coincidence. My cock is six inches—folded in half.* Kinski collects two 3s and two 2s and must X out his full house. Inexplicably, he refuses to call on his conquistador henchmen, Fuck and Asshole. Herzog somehow produces a fifth ace on his final roll, attributing the success to Incan spirits. Claiming his prize, he runs to Kinski's hut, returning with a ½-by-½-inch square of German chocolate precious as a dozen lost gold cities. *Auf Wiedersehen*, Herzog whispers before chomping lustily, a breath from Kinski's face. *You should've pulled the trigger*, Kinski says, exhausted, his face a doomed raft teeming with monkeys.

MEETING POETS (UNRELEASED
BRIAN DEPALMA THRILLER, CA. 1977)

Split-screened, we see through both pairs of eyes
simultaneously. Previous scenes revealed that the
man (Christopher Walken) laughs in his poems but
not in real life, while the Nancy Allen character
is the opposite. While sauntering like only he can,
Walken looks into the pale face of Allen and, smit-
ten, trips on the sidewalk. This looks funny to her
and would seem funny to him on paper. But in
this world, Nancy Allen always dies. Always. Pino
Donaggio's soundtrack will surround the film's
few remaining scenes and edge out comprehen-
sion. Neither Walken nor Allen will be allowed to
write. He will not be able to jot down the phrase
"tripped on the sidewalk," realize he could recast
temporary embarrassment as timeless art. She will
not be able to describe the horror of his sunken
cheeks, the elongated eye contact. The two will
not fall in MPAA-approved love or have airbrushed
sex. They will certainly not write poems together
that compensate for each other's weaknesses. The
director instead creates a simple tryst between
Walken's blade and Allen's throat, a crimson-finale
photocopy that pretends not to need paper.

SQUATCH DOOR
—FOR KRISTIN

They think if you think it will game show, it will.
They are the audience. They see three doors, a man
with a microphone. He wears a Botany 500 suit
while the woman to his left is in pink pants, her
top a polyester floral print. He will ask her to pick
a door. He will ask her to open the door, to walk
through the doorway. Behind one door is a former
model holding a small stack of $100 bills. Behind
another door is a former model holding a large stack
of $1,000 bills. Behind the third door might be Sas-
quatch. If Sasquatch exists, the captors or handlers
of Sasquatch are contractually obligated to posi-
tion Sasquatch behind that door. If Sasquatch does
not exist, and the woman in the pink pants picks
the door potentially destined for Sasquatch, then
the woman gets what exists in Sasquatch's place—
nothing. The real test, the real non–game show
moment, comes when Mrs. Pink Pants realizes she
came all this way for a wee stack of cash, a *grande*
stack of cash, nothing, or a gruesome, sure-thing-
lawsuit death at the hands of a heretofore mythical
beast. These options alone may, in fact, create an
event that transcends the genre.

Brian Wilson Begins to Compose
"Good Vibrations" outside
Dripping Cave, Calif., 1966

Every spring, he chastises Mike Love for bringing
him here. *They have it all wrong,* Wilson says. *It's
always wrong.* He points out the flawed harmonies,
atonalities, how the olive warbler's two-note am-
bulance phrase belongs elsewhere, separated from
that of the towhee, a monotone specialist like that
newcomer Nico but an octave higher. He would
make the marsh wren sit out, its CHICK chick-a-
cha-KAH chicken scratch a bit too James Brown
for the setting. He waits for sage thrashers to rest
a measure as they prattle like old ladies under hair
dryers. Only the kingbird, with its metallic treble,
approximates adequacy. But wait: Amid a drum-
roll trill of wings, a star emerges in the hermit
thrush, which Wilson hadn't identified on previ-
ous visits. He likens himself to Hammond uncov-
ering Holiday, basking in that untapped ache, that
signature phrasing. Wilson now cries out, com-
manding the singing to start over, to open with a
hush of hermit thrushes—four of them. Then the
kingbirds must come in, with purple finches on
background vocals. *You're still not getting it, Mike,*

83

Wilson whines while unfolding a crumpled piece of staff paper, eyeing five lines on which to color the pictures of birds.

JOHN CARPENTER SPLICES TWO OF HIS
RECENT FILMS, LOS ANGELES, 1979

The closing scene lasts all of twenty-five seconds.
A bloated Elvis Presley (Kurt Russell) walks up
to his Graceland bedroom. The camera had been
perched atop the stairs, better to watch Elvis's
struggle to rise. Cut to a reverse shot with heavy
breathing through a cheap mask, a man lumbering
upstairs. The man lifts his right hand in front of
his face so, through his eyes, we can see a knife.
Backed by eerie synthesizer, he pushes a door open.
Cut to Elvis on the bathroom floor, dead in a silk
robe. Now in rapid succession we see Michael
Myers looking dead on a New Jersey lawn, then
a quick shot away, back to the empty space where
Myers lay just seconds ago, and to Elvis, driving
off in a purple Lincoln.

DAVID GREGORY FILLS IN FOR MATT LAUER
ON TODAY, 5/11/07

David Gregory: Will the brioche get too brown?
Martha Stewart: No, the brioche won't get too brown.
DG: How do you know—
MS: Just pay attention. [Laughs]
DG: Right. [Laughs]
MS: Will you make this for your wife on Mother's Day?
DG: Well—
MS: [Laughs]

DG and MS retire to pastel bistro table to eat their French toast.

DG: This is delicious. Truly scrumptious. [Short pause]
What advice do you have for people contemplating insider trading?
Do they serve scrumptious brioche in prison? [Long pause]
Sorry. Force of habit. I used to be... I used to be so... [Clears throat] What was it like babysitting for Mickey Mantle's kids?

MS: I'm so glad you asked that question, David! This brioche is too brown.

THE ANDREW LLOYD WEBBER LECTURE,
COLORADO SPRINGS FINE ARTS CENTER, 4/1/89

Still boyish at barely forty-one, he strides to the
stage in a dreamy gait cribbed from Pink Floyd.
Five hundred pairs of eyes fixate on his lips, which
the fans can't wait to see move. *I flew here on the
golden breath of a* Phantom, he says. Webber waits a
split second too long for the laughter to subside, as
the audience transfers its attention to a man, per-
haps a century old, who has just bumped into a
mobile sculpture. With gnarled, bony fingers, the
man directs the work of art into an asymmetrical
spin. He mouths encouraging words to it, coax-
ing it into somersaults, the haymakers that stifle
speech. This man relies only on pantomime, hav-
ing lost his voice years earlier when he swallowed
too many snowflakes. Meanwhile Webber, not
visibly annoyed, begins to applaud. The others fol-
low his lead as the man bows, then exaggeratedly
tips his cap toward Webber. Holding up a tightly
closed fist, the old man opens his hand to reveal
nothing. He nods broadly at the composer before
exiting into the muted mile-high.

Reading Comprehension Segment from Verbal SAT, 1984

In 1983 A.D., English rock band The Police released the album *Synchronicity*. Pop music's answer to the Sistine Chapel, *Synchronicity* contained sure-thing Number One singles "Every Breath You Take" and "King of Pain," while "Wrapped Around Your Finger" and "Synchonicity II" each peaked at Number Nine on the charts. (To the chagrin of turd lovers, the Andy Summers–warbled "Mother" was not released as a single.) Our masterpiece upstaged an impromptu visit from Christ to win three Grammy Awards.

Giddy as a dislocated knee in a JV basketball scrimmage, *Synchronicity* boldly flaunts its distinctive cover, which depicts band members in mock-irreverent poses topped with electric turquoise, goldenrod, and candy-apple washes of certifiably edgy paint. The three stripes are believed to symbolize the Holy Trinity, the number of members in the band, or front man Stings favorite "soul-portraits" from James Joyce's *A Portrait of the Artist As a Young Man*.

1. The lyric "caught between the Scylla and Charybdis" referred to in "Wrapped Around Your Finger" (line 5) could mean:

   A. Whatever you want it to mean, per Sting's disingenuous advice
   B. The same as the idiom "caught between the devil and the deep blue sea," to which Sting ill-advisedly refers later in the song
   C. You should've listened to Mrs. Kress during the Greek mythology unit so you wouldn't have to spend most of your test time staring up at the gym ceiling
   D. Either way, you're fucked

2. The album's title "Synchronicity" is a reference to:

   A. Carl Jung's theory of the same name
   B. Arthur Koestler's book The *Roots of Coincidence*, which mentions Jung's theory and (surprise, surprise) was one of Sting's favorite works of highbrow esotericism

C. The chance that two events—e.g., the birth of Sting and the Netherlands' launch of its first national television station on October 2, 1951—could share no causal relationship but nonetheless happen together in a deeply meaningful way

D. The chance that you will be compelled to look up nerve-racking, obscure literary references while listening to a Police song

3. It is clear Sting "will always be king of pain" (line 5) because:

A. It was prophesied in the Ayn Rand novel *Atlas Shrugged*

B. "Caribbean Queen" singer Billy Ocean named him such because the then-earthbound Gordon Sumner was wearing a black-and-gold sweater, and Pretentious Asshole Who Looks Like a Fucking Bee in That Shit Sweater was slightly unwieldy

C. Morrissey just doesn't have what it takes

D. There's always community college

STOP

ABOUT THE AUTHOR

Daniel M. Shapiro is a schoolteacher who lives in Pittsburgh. He is the author of three poetry chapbooks and a collection of collaborations with Jessy Randall.